CONVERSATIONS ABOUT GOD AND THE PROBLEM OF EVIL

GRAHAM OPPY
SAM LEBENS

INTERVIEWED BY

JASON WERBELOFF
MARK OPPENHEIMER

OBSIDIAN WORLDS PUBLISHING

Conversations about God and the Problem of Evil
Copyright: Jason Keith Werbeloff, Mark Oppenheimer,
Graham Oppy, Sam Lebens
Editor: Yolande Coetser
Publisher: Obsidian Worlds Publishing, Johannesburg,
South Africa
Published: 1 December 2021

CONTENTS

FOREWORD

Let's do what forewords do. First, express that I'm delighted and honored to write this foreword: I'm delighted and honored to write the foreword of this book by four pals—Jason Werbeloff, Mark Oppenheimer, Graham Oppy and Sam Lebens.

Second, introduce the authors: Jason is one of the sharpest philosophical talents I know. He never pursued an academic career. What is philosophy's loss is science fiction's gain. He's one of my favorite authors. You should buy his novels now. Mark is one of the sharpest legal talents around, and is a prominent South African constitutional advocate and media personality. I have no idea whether he is related to the mining magnate Oppenheimer family.

Graham is a preeminent atheist philosopher of religion.

He lives near the beach in Australia. Sam is a preeminent Jewish philosopher of religion. He lives near the beach in Israel. I've spent some time on the beach with Sam. Hanging out with Jason, Mark, Sam and Graham on the beach would be close to heaven. The plane tickets, hotels and drinks would be on Mark.

I was friends with Jason and Mark way back when we were undergraduate students in South Africa. I've worked with both Graham and Sam on various academic projects. I've authored a lot with Sam not so way back when I was a philosophy professor, and he remains one of my best friends (though it's a low bar, since I don't have many friends).

I don't recall introducing them all, and attribute our appearing together here to divine providence. Graham, are you convinced *now*?

Third, praise the book: With such a distinguished line up, you likely won't be disappointed! The book is friendly and insightful, and has one of the most important virtues of any book—it's short.

Fourth, summarize the book: The book includes two interviews based on Jason and Mark's podcasts with the authors about God and evil. The first interview is with Graham, and starts with the problem of evil: how could a perfectly good God allow all the bad stuff around? Graham introduces the atheistic argument based on this problem as well as theistic responses to it. He then goes on to consider arguments for the existence of God as well as atheistic responses to those. While Graham is an atheist, he doesn't think we currently have any philosophical arguments that should move a reasonable audience in either direction.

The next interview is with Sam, and focuses entirely on the problem of evil. Sam outlines a new response to the problem of evil that we developed together and published a few years ago. The idea is that God might destroy all past, present and future evils. He might remove all the wrongdoing and suffering from history. Not just the history books, but from history itself: one day it will be the case that there never ever was any war or a disease. Making sense of this requires some careful thinking about the nature of time and God's power of it.

Graham does not address this answer to the problem of evil in his interview, and Sam does not address the theistic arguments or the prospects of arguments generally in his interview. I hope that this book sparks their interest in publishing an extended dialogue together on these topics, and I hope that it sparks the readers interest in pursuing the questions further themselves. Which brings me to the next thing a foreword might do.

Fifth, recommend further reading: For general introductory books:

> Zagzebski, Linda (2007). *The Philosophy of Religion: An Historical Introduction.* Wiley-Blackwell — a general philosophy of religion textbook

> Nagasawa, Yujin (2011). *The Existence of God: A Philosophical Introduction.* Routledge — an impartial introduction to classical arguments for the existence of God

> Swinburne, Richard (2010). *Is There a God?* Oxford University Press — an accessible and elegant defense of arguments for the existence of God

> Frances, Bryan (2013). *Gratuitous Suffering and the Problem of Evil: A Comprehensive*

Introduction. Routledge — an accessible and engaging defense of the argument from evil against the existence of God

For more advanced books:

Swinburne, Richard (2004). *The Existence of God*. Oxford University Press — likely the most sophisticated arguments for the existence of God

Oppy, Graham (2006). *Arguing About Gods*. Cambridge University Press — likely the most sophisticated critique of arguments for the existence of God

Stump, Eleonore (2010). *Wandering in Darkness: Narrative and the Problem of Suffering*. Oxford University Press — likely the most sophisticated response to the problem of evil from a Christian philosopher

Lebens, Sam (2020). *The Principles of Judaism*. Oxford, UK: Oxford University Press — likely the most sophisticated philosophical treatment of the principles of Judaism

For readers who especially liked the dialogue format of this book:

Hume, David (1998/1779). *Dialogues Concerning Natural Religion* — a classical and beautiful skeptical book by the greatest philosophical skeptic

Perry, John (1999). *Dialogue on Good, Evil, and the Existence of God*. Hackett Publishing Company — a short introduction to the problem of evil by one of the smartest contemporary philosophers

Alter, Torin & Robert Howell (2011). *The God Dialogues: A Philosophical Journey*. Oxford University Press — a thorough and impartial introduction to philosophy of religion

TYRON GOLDSCHMIDT

November 2021

The Problem of Evil

Graham Oppy

Imagine that you are travelling to a new kingdom. The reputation of the kingdom is that it is ruled by a benevolent, wise and powerful king who ensures that it is a wonderful place. From a distance, the kingdom looks glorious – not very big, but situated in green rolling fields, cities shining in the sun. As you cross the border, you are filled with high expectations. However, as you proceed, you realise with horror that bodies of men, women, and children are hanging from the lampposts along the route you are walking.

And so you reconsider. It does not seem like it can be true that the kingdom is ruled by a powerful, wise and benevolent ruler. Perhaps this is an outlying area and the ruler does not know. But this means that the ruler is not well informed, implying that he is perhaps not as wise as he was reported to be. It could also be that he knows about the killings, but he can do nothing to prevent them. So maybe he is actually not powerful. Furthermore, it might be that he knows about the bodies and he could prevent the killings, but he does nothing. If this is the case, we can conclude that he is not so good. Maybe he is morally indifferent and does not care. Even worse, maybe he is responsible for the killings.

It has become clear that the kingdom is not under the control of a ruler who is all-powerful, all-wise, and benevolent.

If one finds oneself in those circumstances, you should conclude that the ruler does not satisfy the initial description that you were given as you entered the kingdom.

JASON WERBELOFF

Your thought experiment seems to be an analogy to God and the idea that he is all-good, all-knowing and all-powerful. And the analogy is that if this sovereign being who is responsible for creating the world is actually all-good, all-knowing and all-powerful, then we would not expect to see the evils and suffering that we see daily. The people hanging from the lampposts are analogous to the evils and suffering we see daily – people dying, the Covid pandemic, and other evils. The conclusion can be reached, as with the thought experiment, that there simply cannot be such a being, or if there is such a being, that he is not all-good, all-powerful, or all-knowing.

GRAHAM OPPY

A year ago I would have rather used the various genocides of the 20th Century as examples, like the Belgians in the Congo and others all over the world. But yes, you are right – the claim that our world is ruled by an all-powerful, all-knowing, and all-good God is challenged by the evidence of, for example, the Covid-pandemic, in the same way, that the bodies hanging from the lampposts challenge the idea of the wise, knowing and benevolent ruler of the kingdom.

MARK OPPENHEIMER

Two different kinds of evils are described. The first are those performed by free agents – when people go out and murder and rape and commit genocides. But then there is a second kind of evil, natural evil, like earthquakes, tsunamis, and the Covid pandemic. The theist might respond and say that it is important for people to have free will and that God surrenders to the greater good by allowing people to have free will and by not interfering with that free will.

Do you think the theist can use a similar argument about the natural evils, which have nothing to do with a free agent?

GRAHAM OPPY

Let's return to the initial thought experiment. It does not seem very compelling for the sovereign to say "yes, I know about the killings, and I agree that it is bad, and, while I can stop it, I won't, since there are people who want to do it and I think it is important to let them make their own choices about what to do."

There seems to be a limit to the amount of freedom that should be granted. For example, the criminal justice system should lock up perpetrators so the rest of can be protected from being hung up from lampposts.

We can also question the importance of freedom, especially in light of the ruler – is freedom so important that it justifies inaction on the part of the sovereign? The same might be true of God: in the face of genocide, the good of freedom is simply insufficient to justify inaction of God's part.

But that still leaves us with the question about natural evils – hurricanes, tornadoes and pandemics. We can also consider animal suffering – for the last three to five hundred million years, an enormous amount of animals have experienced suffering that has very little to do with humans since humans have only been around for a fraction of that time. We need a different story than the free will of humans that will tell us why the ruler of the universe set up things to allow such an incredibly long history of suffering.

JASON WERBELOFF

We might therefore conclude that free will not help us to explain suffering. But, maybe the analogy is wrong – perhaps it problematic to compare the sovereign and God, since God may be more knowledgeable than any sovereign could ever be. It could be that God can foresee a reason why suffering is taking place in a way that the sovereign cannot. There might be some mysterious reason why animals and people need to suffer which may rest in some good that we are unaware of.

GRAHAM OPPY

That is a more promising line of argumentation for a theist to take. You do not necessarily have to put the possible goods far into the future, you could simply argue that there are goods that depend on the suffering taking place. Put differently, certain goods might arise from suffering, and we have trouble seeing those goods given that there is an omnipotent, omniscient, and good God in control. At first glance, this seems a difficult argument to counter. But, let us consider some really awful suffering like the torture of a child who subsequently dies. How plausible is it that there is a good for the child that arises out of the suffering and the dying? It is not enough that there be good for somebody else or something else. That cannot justify the torture and suffering of the child. But where does the child get the good and how does it get it? How can it possibly be that there is some good for the child that depends upon their being tortured and killed? That seems really hard to believe.

MARK OPPENHEIMER

The theist has a few options here. The one is to appeal to further supernatural entities. The argument could go something like "this world may be full of all this immense suffering but do not worry there is an afterlife where you get to bathe in the glory of God and it is an eternity of absolute splendour." That would mean that all the suffering that took place pales in significance – it was good for the child to die, because of the grand plan.

The other option is to appeal to a utilitarian account of morality. God might allow people to be killed for the greater good.

The third move is for the theist to argue that whatever God does by nature is good because it is done by God, and so any kind of human moral account is irrelevant.

GRAHAM OPPY

We must be careful not to underplay the awfulness of the suffering of the child, so weighting goods is not a good argument, even if what follows is really great. It is very hard to see what the child would be missing out on by not being tortured and murdered – that is an odd way to set things up.

There are various questions about the afterlife. But if in the afterlife there is no suffering and there is only good stuff, then why not just make that and skip the rest of it. That is a bit hard to fathom. Even if God was a utilitarian, for the reasons I just gave it is unclear how you are going to get a justification for the torture and murder of the child because it is unclear how to get the goodness in the later state to depend on that.

MARK OPPENHEIMER

The theist could respond and say that you simply have an incorrect account of goodness when you say a bad thing happened to the tortured and murdered child. Because it happened under the auspice of God it was necessarily good. The theist will say you have a human understanding of morality, and the theist talks about a godly kind of morality when she talks about a benevolent God.

GRAHAM OPPY

We have a shared opinion that the torture and murder

of a child is a terrible thing. If God's morality says something other than that, then it is a black mark against God. Then God cannot possibly be perfectly good. Maybe God is morally indifferent. Maybe God is evil. But it has to be that if you are in a position where you can prevent the torture and murder of a small child at no costs to yourself then you should do it. We would expect nothing less of people. I think you are going to struggle to make it plausible that we should be calling God good if somehow or other God's moral views, if you can call them that, endorse just letting children be tortured and killed.

JASON WERBELOFF

Suppose the theist doubles down on her argument by suggesting again, that, since God is by definition good, whatever God does is good too. The theist could say that you simply cannot fathom it with your puny human mind, but that God knows and since God ordained that that child is tortured and murdered, it is good.

GRAHAM OPPY

That does not sound very plausible to me. A question I would like to ask the theist then is how much more suffering do you need before you decide that there is too much suffering in the world. How many more hundred million years of animals suffering do you need or how many more children do you need to be tortured and killed before you are going to go back from the position that you have just taken up. Do you think that no matter how bad the world was, it could not possibly count as evidence against there being a good creator?

MARK OPPENHEIMER

You allude to the problem of evil being used as an argument against the existence of God. But, it might just argue against the existence of a certain kind of God. We could imagine a deist God who created everything, sets the wheels in motion and then withdraws. Whatever evil or suffering happens, this God does not get involved. This God is not omnibenevolent but is nevertheless a God.

GRAHAM OPPY

You have several options in responding to the argument as you have set it up. You could reduce the amount of power that you attribute to God, or you could reduce the amount of knowledge. Or, you could reduce him out of goodness. If you reduce any one or all three of these enough, then perhaps you can justify the suffering.

Your deist God might make the world, and then goes on to doing something else. The deist God is not awful; it just does what it does – it makes universes one after the other to see how they turn out.

It could also be that there are two possible Gods. One is good, and one is evil, and they are equally powerful. You, therefore, get a universe that has lots of good things and lots of bad things, because there are two opposing Gods at war with each other in the world they have created. That was historically a popular view, but then with the advent of Christianity, it became heresy. But, it was not an unpopular view in the ancient world.

We could also imagine that perhaps God is not as powerful as we might think. God knows what is going on and cares about it, but cannot do anything about it.

But there are all these options and it does not look as though any considerations about the ambits and kinds of evils in the world are going to refute them: The thing that is supposed to be refuted here is the idea that there is an omnipotent, omniscient, perfectly good God.

JASON WERBELOFF

I prefer a pantheistic solution.

With theism, God is an all-good, all-knowing and all-powerful agent who can do things about evil. He knows about evil, and he wants to do something about it, because he is good, and he has the power to do something about it. We conclude that he should then do something about it.

With pantheism, God is not an agent, and he did not create the universe. Rather, he *is* the universe. The universe and God are identical.

Represented on a diagram, theism sees God as a larger circle, with the universe a smaller circle inside that circle. Pantheism also allows for the existence of evil, since evil is part of the universe, along with all other things, and it is all identical with God. You, therefore, do not have the problem of justifying why and how God is all good, all-knowing and all-powerful because God is not an agent.

GRAHAM OPPY

There are other views that you could take as well. You might think of God as impersonal but not pantheistic, like Brahman. There are various eastern religions where things that look more like principles than people are the fundamental object of the religion. These conceptions do not look like they are particularly threatened by the problem of evil.

JASON WERBELOFF

I have two clarifying questions. The first relates to the term 'evil', which philosophers might use differently from the way people use the term in everyday settings. Could you perhaps say more about this?

The second question is whether you think the existence of evil is logically inconsistent with the existence of God as an all-good, all-knowing, all-powerful person? Or rather, do you think that the problem of evil provides inductive or abductive evidence against the existence of God? By inductive or abductive I mean that it provides probable rather than conclusive deductive evidence.

GRAHAM OPPY

To answer your first question, we know that some people define evil as an affront to God, entailing that if there is no God, then there is no evil. That is definitely not the way that philosophers think about evil.

A different view is that evil constitutes really horrendously bad things: mild experience of pain need not constitute evil in this view. This is not how philosophers typically think about evil.

Here is one reason why philosophers think about evil in a way that allows that even mild experiences of pain are evils. At the beginning of the theistic story, there was perfection and nothing else. Later, we start seeing imperfection. So, we might think of imperfection as an evil. However, then you have the problem of how you get imperfection from perfection. This problem is underrated – it is hard to understand how that could have happened. But that gives one a sense that evil can be understood as anything which is a departure from perfection.

Your second question is about the form of the argument. Some people think that there is a logical inconsistency between facts about evil (like evil exists, or there is horrendous evil, or a lot of evil), facts about God (like that he is omnipotent, omniscient, and perfectly good), and some further facts connecting facts about God and facts about evil. Per illustration, John Mackie thought that there is a contradiction involving the mere existence of evil, God's omnipotence and omnibenevolence, and thehe further claims that an omnipotent being has no limits to what it can do, and that a benevolent being would eliminate evil as far as he could. These claims taken together gives us a contradiction.

There are other arguments which claim, not that there is a logical contradiction, but rather that the best explanation for the evil in the world is that there is no such thing as an omnipotent, omniscient and perfectly good being. We can infer from the evils we see that there is no omnipotent, omniscient, perfectly good God.

There are more complicated arguments – you can add more attributes and perhaps add more detailed facts about evil.

If we go back to Mackie's argument, I do not think that the two linking premises that he had are true. If that was your argument, then you would have an easy out – we could just say that there are limits to what an omnipotent being can do. They cannot do what is impossible, so, you cannot have certain kinds of good without evils. For example, you cannot overcome adversity without adversity, and the overcoming of adversity is a good thing. If you have neither the adversity nor the overcoming of adversity, then you cannot have the good of overcoming adversity.

Mackie's argument does not succeed. I do not think there is any other logical argument that works better than that one. There are better arguments than Mackie's, but I am convinced that none of them is any more successful.

MARK OPPENHEIMER

You alluded to the fact that we have different ways of trying to explain the world that we live in. We can accept that we live in a world with lots of suffering and some pleasure. We have a choice between a world where we posit a supernatural deity and one where we say there is not such a deity. Are there any reasons to prefer one account over the other?

GRAHAM OPPY

I do not think there is a deity – all that there is, is a natural reality, at least as far as causality goes. We can simplify the views about contemporary cosmology by saying that the universe is all there is. Within this world, life emerged and there is a long period of evolution that involved competing for resources, which makes animal suffering inevitable. We can therefore make sense of animal suffering from a naturalist hypothesis.

From a theistic perspective, however, it is hard to find a good reason to explain suffering. We can postulate that there are goods that we simply do not know about that God has in mind when he allows suffering. But that adds more stuff to the story. You have the universe. You have God. You have these unknown goods. But the theists cannot agree on, or they might not know, why God lets the animals suffer.

Good and evil fit quite naturally in the naturalist story, and that gives us a reason for preferring the naturalist hypothesis and rejecting the theist hypothesis. This is, however, just one reason – to make a judgement about either position, one should weigh up different types of evidence. Nevertheless, if we just focus on the problem of evil, then the naturalist view is favoured.

MARK OPPENHEIMER

What are the best arguments that the theist has for believing their version over the naturalist's account?

GRAHAM OPPY

Different kinds of arguments have been popular during different times in the last thousand years. There was a time when cosmological arguments were all the rage, then there was a period when it was arguments from design, then there was a period when it was moral arguments.

Let us consider the cosmological argument – why is there a universe at all? What could possibly explain the existence of the universe? Theists have an answer to these questions: God made it. It is not so clear what the naturalist might say, since they do not think that there is an external cause of the universe. If the universe is all there is, the naturalist cannot provide a causal explanation.

It seems that the theist can explain something that the naturalist cannot – the existence of the universe.

JASON WERBELOFF

I think it was Nagel who said that you are asking for one explanation too many. So, we can cite the big bang as the reason for the existence of the universe, which seems to be good enough, and if you ask what caused the big bang, then you are asking for one explanation too many.

GRAHAM OPPY

The question is how to think about the beginning point. The 'big bang' is a vague label for some stuff that we do not know very much about. We have a pretty accurate theory about what happened thereafter – the period of inflation right after the big bang – but before that, we are in uncharted territory. We have no evidence or theories that explain the existence of the universe back then. But if we assume we have a series of states, where did that first state come from? It does not seem to be asking for one explanation too many, since all the other states have explanations. We explain all the states in terms of earlier states, but then when we get back to the first state, it is not clear that there is anything special about that first state that does not need an explanation.

My own preference is to say that the first state was necessary – it could not have been otherwise. Theists would say the same thing – that God made the first state, and that God exists because he must.

This argument takes the advantage away from the theist since we have both gotten to the initial thing that exists out of necessity. But the theists have taken it an extra step, and so Nagel might be right – it is a step too far.

MARK OPPENHEIMER

The fine-tuning arguments are also popular – the notion that the universe is calibrated in such a manner that if one of the many laws of the universe were slightly off the whole thing would not be there. This does not appear to be random, rather, it looks like the kind of sophisticated system made a creator. The argument is that the creator applied its wisdom to calibrating everything so perfectly and that since this is unlikely to have occurred without a creator, we, therefore, posit a creator.

GRAHAM OPPY

We can ask a few questions about physics at this point. We do not have finished physics, in fact, physics is in an unsatisfactory state because we have two superb theories – quantum mechanics and general relativity – that are inconsistent with one another. Since early in the 20th Century, physicists have been looking for some Grand Unified Theory that would unite quantum mechanics and general relativity together in a coherent way – but we do not have that.

One of the things we do not know is whether there will be all of these finally calibrated values in the successor theory. In the theories we have now, you have to put values in by hand and their precision really matters. If you vary them just a little bit, then it looks like the universe will simply blow up instantly and consist of nothing but empty space or it collapses in on itself in a fraction of a second. So there is no chance for life to emerge.

We do not know what the future of physics is going to look like. But, if we put that aside and we suppose that in the future physics will have all of these values that go in by hand, then several questions remain. One question is where in the evolution of the universe these values get fixed. There are two possible answers – either they are fixed in the beginning or there is a point where values go from not being fixed to being fixed. If there is such a transition, then there is nothing left for the naturalist to explain – there is simply an evolution where there is a phase transition where values get fixed. It is a matter of chance which values you end up with. If, on the other hand, values are fixed in the beginning, that state is necessary and there are no alternatives – the values had to be as they are. That would be the consequence of such a view. One line of argument is that the values have been that way since the beginning, and it happened by chance, and there is nothing wrong with that. There are lots of naturalists who say "I do not like either of those options." One popular response is that there are multiple universes and values get set randomly in these universes. There are lots of universes that blow up or collapse fairly quickly, but, because there are so many universes, some of them have values that are just right for life. And our universe is one where the values are right for life. This is a response that I would prefer to avoid, but that is one option to explain the existence of life.

JASON WERBELOFF

There is a problem with the view that the starting state of the universe is necessary. If we combine the view that the starting state is necessary with the view that the world is determined, then there is only one outcome – you have an entirely deterministic universe. Our intuition, however, is that the world could have been different, which is at odds with a deterministic universe.

GRAHAM OPPY

One would only go for this view if you also accept the view that the state transition is indeterministic, which is a view I favour. There are two reasons at least why you might favour that view. One is that quantum mechanics suggest that the world is indeterministic. Not every interpretation of quantum mechanics does, but most of the plausible ones do. The other thing is that if you want to suppose that there is free will (of the libertarian kind), then the transitions have to be indeterministic. I am more persuaded by the quantum mechanical consideration. Either way, to take my view, you have to accept that there is indeterminism. This view does not come from thinking about God, but rather from thinking about modality.

A nice theory of modality would be one where every possible world shares some history with the actual world, and you get divergences only because chances play out differently. That gives you a very neat theory of modality. However, it has fewer possibilities than most people think there are. It also makes it very hard to work out what is possible and what is not.

JASON WERBELOFF

I really like the idea of other possible worlds with different sets of laws of nature. I am a science fiction writer, so that intrigues me. But on your view, that would not be possible because the laws of nature would be part of that initial state that is necessary.

GRAHAM OPPY

This is a metaphysical necessity, but we still have metaphysical possibility, imaginative possibility, doxastic possibility, that we can believe in. What is possible given the evidence that we have got thus far? Nothing will stop you from writing science fiction stories, but the consequence is that there are not metaphysical possibilities on these views.

MARK OPPENHEIMER

Richard Dawkins countered the fine-tuning argument – if we think about the universe as a perfectly calibrated hi-fi set, where all the levels have to be at the correct numbers for it to work probably. The inference is that there has to be something turning the knobs – a Divine Knob-Twiddler. However, this being has to be highly complicated since it has the ability to set the hi-fi system in motion. To get out of a complicated problem, we created a further complicated problem for ourselves – we have not explained the existence of this infinitely impressive being that can make universes.

GRAHAM OPPY

There has to be some complexity in the background since there is something with an incredibly detailed plan, that has weighed up all these alternative possibilities. If they set all the knobs up in this way, then there will be a universe with life. And that sounds very complicated.

What theists will say, though, is that the being that has the plan is simple even though the plan is obviously highly complex. And you might wonder how a simple being could have such a complex plan and to that extent Dawkins might be right. But theists typically seem not very moved by the Dawkins argument in my experience. There is, something rather simple about supposing that God is infinitely wise and infinitely powerful and infinitely good. There are no limitations on God. And if you are an unlimited being it is going to be easy for you to get the dials just right.

MARK OPPENHEIMER

I wonder about Occam's razor and its ability to persuade people. The philosopher says we must prefer simple accounts. But there is an ambiguity there. Someone who is raised a theist will say their account is simple, and that a non-theist account seems complicated since it relies on complicated physics. The God answer seems simple. There is some equivocation of the term 'simple' here. I wonder if you had thoughts about that.

The other question is one about methods of persuasion: in other words, are there better or worse ways to have this conversation?

GRAHAM OPPY

The question about simplicity is tricky. If you have

read Richard Swinburne's book, *The Existence of God*, you will know that he makes a lot of simplicity judgments in setting up his cumulative argument for God, which is quite similar to my own argument. And he thinks that the simple measures are zero, one, and infinity. As long as you are attaching those quantities to aspects of God then you are coming up with something really simple. I do not think that is a good account of simplicity. What I offer in its place may not seem much better, so perhaps we ought to think about theories.

Think about theories as sets of senses. If we compare the beliefs of the theist and the non-theist, then we should have two consistent stories that conflict in a variety of ways.

Then there will be two questions. One question is about which account is simpler, the other one is about which account fits the data that we agree on better. The nature of the data is not too important here.

So let us think about simplicity. There are at least three dimensions.

One is about the different kinds of things that exist. The second is what ideas you know to express the theory - the fewer ideas needed, the simpler it is. The third thing is if you axiomatise the theories, which one ends up with the smallest, neatest set of axioms. These are all dimensions of simplicity. The tricky thing is knowing how to weigh them. The best theory is one that makes the best trade-off between minimising new commitments (i.e. becoming simpler) and explaining as much as possible. We do not measure those things separately, but rather together to work out which is the better theory.

Now that is not a nice, clean, simple story. It is nothing as simple as zero, one or infinity. But it seems to me to do a better job of explaining what we are talking about.

JASON WERBELOFF

The theist is going to say that is not a simple explanation of what simplicity is.

GRAHAM OPPY

That is true; it was not very simple. I am relying on ideas about theory choice that I have borrowed from philosophy of science, and incorporated that into philosophy of religion.

MARK OPPENHEIMER

If we think about Peter Boghossian's view about how to have impossible conversations, and his book *A Manual for Creating Atheists*, then we see that he thinks that there is a certain way that theists and atheists should talk that is more likely to lead to progress in the conversation. Often these sorts of conversations can be quite militant and neither side sees each other.

GRAHAM OPPY

The really hard thing to do if you want to have productive conversations with people is to think yourself into their position. If you can figure out enough about how they see the world, then you start being able to predict what they are going to say, then you are much closer to having productive conversations. Part of having productive conversations is just being civil and interested and actually taking the time to read and talk with people who hold different views from your own. That happens in corners of the internet – I am all for productive conversations, rather than debates, where people just present their own views without exchange. It is much more interesting to talk to people and draw out of them questions and comments. And I think that is how philosophers who are theists, and naturalists discussing God should conduct themselves.

MARK OPPENHEIMER

Have you seen moments of doubt in those conversations? In other words, where the theist admits to hearing something which sees her doubting, and similarly where the atheist considers that God might exist?

GRAHAM OPPY

I have not seen either of those things. But what I have seen "Oh, that is interesting; maybe my view about X is not quite right". Any book defending naturalism or theism has thousands of controversial claims and very few authors will think that they are right about all of those claims. Most consider that their views could be improved and that there are ways in which they might be getting things wrong. Often, the conversation takes the form of pointing out incompatibilities in a position, and the other person acknowledging that and going to think about it.

JASON WERBELOFF

Suppose you have two rational people – one is a theist

and one is an atheist. These people have an infinite amount of time. Are there arguments that you think should convince one of those sides?

GRAHAM OPPY

I do not think we currently have any arguments that should convince either of them to budge. But that does not rule out there being arguments that we have not been clever enough to discover yet but could convince either side. That is my position on most of the kinds of arguments that there are.

I wrote a fairly big book back in the last decade where I argued that there are no successful arguments on either side. But I made it very clear that what I meant was we do not *currently* have them. None of the arguments that have been written down, that we have examined, are persuasive. I also do not think we will find such a convincing argument any time soon. But, we cannot rule out such a killer argument emerging on either side.

JASON WERBELOFF

Are you a pragmatic agnostic?

GRAHAM OPPY

I do not think so. I do not think that argument is as important as theory. In fact, I think that what you say about the arguments is entirely determined by the theory that you hold. I judge that naturalism does a better job than theism of managing all of the relevant evidence. You invest in less and you get more explanation.

But it is a very complicated judgment and reasonable people can disagree about lots of the sub-judgments that go into that overall judgment. I am quite happy to think some smart, intelligent, well-informed people could disagree with me about some of the particular judgments and the judgment overall.

If one day we find the killer argument, then we will have something to fall back on. But I would not count on that. I guess that the situation will go on and people must figure it out for themselves. There are lots of philosophies. Most of the big questions, questions about consciousness, or freedom, or rights have a spectrum of views that reasonable people can hold. We have got no way of forcing all the reasonable people to adopt one particular position. I do not see why we should think that the question about God is any different from other philosophical questions in that respect.

MARK OPPENHEIMER

Do you think that there are degrees of reasonable views on this front? We talked about the ordinary theistic model, and then pantheism. When we were weighing up these accounts, are there any that seem beyond the scope of reason?

GRAHAM OPPY

I think what the pantheist wants to say is that there is the property of being worthy of worship, and that the universe has this property, but that the naturalists do not recognise this property.

But, it is hard to rule things out. In philosophy, positions are often popular, and they go out of vogue, and people think those positions will never be popular again, but things can change. Per illustration, for the first time in almost a century, metaphysical idealism is generating interest again. The history of philosophy is full of examples like these.

While philosophers might consider their position better than the alternatives, that is no reason to think that there are not a huge range of other reasonable views.

JASON WERBELOFF

The non-philosopher might object, and say that if there is a huge range of views and no conclusive reason for eliminating any of them, then how will the philosopher make any progress, especially when her idea loses fashionability, just to regain it again later? Is there ever really progress?

GRAHAM OPPY

There are a bunch of disciplines and for each discipline, there is a core of stuff that is agreed on by experts – the stuff that you just have to know to be competent in a discipline. But there is also the stuff that people are currently working on, and, while they might have some tentative solutions, they do not yet have conclusive solutions. Then you have those questions that people have no idea how to approach – no idea of method or if it even is an answerable question. Now you are in the domain of philosophy.

Philosophy is the domain where there is just no expert agreement on the results of methods or anything like that. How does philosophy make progress? It turns into other things. There was natural philosophy and then there is a period where some progress is made and suddenly you have got physics. For a while logic was on the cusp of becoming an independent discipline, and it was only after the Second World War that it did. My view is that philosophy is really hard, and we struggle with problems, and sometimes we have successes and then we do not get credit for that because now it is called psychology or physics or chemistry. But philosophers should not give up.

MARK OPPENHEIMER

In a way, you are saying that progress happens when something becomes incontrovertible and no longer of interest to philosophers. Philosophers do not like to argue about that which can get a clear answer. Philosophers look at the unknown, and so we are like space explorers, looking out for the stuff that we do not understand yet. There is still a lot that we do not understand, but that is where the fun lies.

GRAHAM OPPY

It is important to think about things on the edges of disciplines that exist. A recent change in philosophy is that many philosophers will have another degree and actually have experience in another discipline. For instance, a philosopher of physics will not just sit in an armchair but will talk to physicists about the boundary problems, the questions that no one knows what to do with.

MARK OPPENHEIMER

Similarly, with ethics, where traditionally philosophers have sat in armchairs thinking about people's intuitions. Now, you have experimental philosophers who survey people to find out what they *actually* believe. This raises an interesting question about whether the philosopher should also be doing more empirical work.

GRAHAM OPPY

Philosophers have often made claims about what ordinary people think. I think that we should do research to find out what ordinary people think. And so I am all for experimental philosophy. Going out and getting relevant results. It is dangerous to make generalisations about what people think. But it is particularly dangerous to do it if you do not have any data.

JASON WERBELOFF

Could that not reduce philosophy to a question of popularity? It might result in the most popular views being seen as the 'correct' views. We do not think that philosophy should be decided on popularity, but rather by rational people.

GRAHAM OPPY

I was not saying that ethics should be decided in that way – I was simply thinking about the range of opinions that can reasonably be held by people. It might be that people believe something unimaginable to us since we just could not imagine the other beliefs they hold alongside that belief.

We will never decide normative questions by popularity polls. In particular, the questions that we are going to answer by doing experimental philosophy on ethical intuitions are not going to be the normative questions.

But that does not mean they are not going to be legitimate questions that we can probe using that technique.

MARK OPPENHEIMER

What are the areas in philosophy of religion where there are open questions that still need to be discovered? What is the next book that you would like to work on?

GRAHAM OPPY

The next book that I write will not be in philosophy of religion, but it will bear on philosophy of religion. I have been thinking about the arguments about the existence of God forever. I would like to write a book about the theory I have come to, based on years of dealing with these arguments about the existence of God. I do not think anyone is going to like it, but that is what I want to do next.

Another project I would like to do is on the history of atheism. I want to know why atheism emerged in France in the early 18th century. What happened between the year 1000 and the year 1729 that made it possible for atheism to emerge? In 1697 Thomas

Aikenhead was a student at Edinburgh University who was put to death for persistent public affirmation of atheism. By 1770 there is a doctor in the UK who puts his name on a pamphlet defining atheism and nobody touches him. The world changed enormously in a small amount of time. But there is a very long run-up to that and I would like to understand what happened in the UK and Europe that made this transition possible. I am not a historian, but I would like to do that.

MARK OPPENHEIMER

Views on atheism have shifted very dramatically in the last twenty years. It has become less popular to be a theist on campuses nowadays. Being religious is going to be more the subject of ridicule than being an atheist. In Sweden, they polled people under the age of 25 and found that there were no theists. Why has atheism garnered so much recent support?

GRAHAM OPPY

Even in the United States, there are fewer churchgoers under 30 than there used to be. In the West, atheism seems to be increasing. In the 1900 Australian census, there were only three percent who were not Christian. The next census will be the first one when more than

GRAHAM OPPY, SAM LEBENS, JASON WERBELOFF, MARK OPPENHEIMER

50 per cent of people are not Christian in Australia. So the change is quite dramatic and it is happening everywhere in a certain part of the world. There are lots of hard questions about why that is happening. What explains it? That will be a job for somebody else.

JASON WERBELOFF

I can imagine views shifting now as well, given that we have gone through a world-altering pandemic. I can imagine a lot of people changing their minds about the existence of God based on some view of evil. They might think that something bad has happened which we did not think was consistent with the idea of a benevolent God. People's views might shift because of a far-reaching event.

GRAHAM OPPY

It is true and we did witness some of that. After the Second World War, in Jewish populations, the holocaust did lead to a loss of faith for a lot of people. I assume that that was true amongst Christians as well, especially having the two world wars so close to one another. But even in the 20th century, there were ups and downs. In the United States, there was something of a resurgence in Christianity during the 50s and early

60s. Maybe it is to do with the cold war and the kind of identification of being an American with being Christian that somehow was stitched together at the time.

Although, from the beginning of the 19th century it is mostly an upward trend for atheism in the countries that we are talking about. I do not know that I would be that confident predicting what things will look like in 50 years. We are weird creatures is what I would say.

MARK OPPENHEIMER

Do you think the rise in atheism has led to a different kind of vacuum? Religious people tend to not just have commitments to deities but also commitment towards certain moral attitudes. Atheists can have a series of other moral commitments. They can be Kantians or utilitarians.

It seems to be, on campuses at least, there is a rise in atheism and then a replacement theology that happens: another kind of belief in an original sin and that a lot of religious language gets used without belief in deities and that original sin might be something like being a coloniser.

South Africa and Australia are both colonies of the UK, and maybe there is a view that being a coloniser is to have original sin.

GRAHAM OPPY

Religious people often say that there is nothing original in atheists. Atheists just borrow stuff from religion, stealing arguments from the *disputatios*. I do not think that is right, but it might be that it is much harder to have this large scale repudiation of pre-existing religious beliefs than you might have thought. Maybe there is something to the idea that you find these patterns of thought that are not really consistent with naturalism but are consistent with at least temporarily walking away from whatever the predominant religions were. Naturalism is still quite an extreme position. I think there aren't lots of naturalists out there. The data suggests for example that even amongst the Swedes many people are not naturalists even though they are not Christians and even though they claim that they are not religious at all.

MARK OPPENHEIMER

It seems like there is a rise in atheists who are not naturalists – so they might not believe in God, but perhaps in something like the universe providing for things, or angels. There is not, therefore, a total overlap between naturalists and atheists.

GRAHAM OPPY

I suspect most people who are atheists are not also naturalists – but the survey data is terrible and censuses and surveys do not distinguish between the different types of non-theists like atheists, agnostics, spiritual people, and people who have no religion. Even then, the term 'naturalist' might not be known amongst atheists, and so they might not even know if they should call themselves that.

JASON WERBELOFF

By atheism, you, therefore, just mean the view that theism is false?

GRAHAM OPPY

Yes.

JASON WERBELOFF

A naturalist position would be a lot stronger than just the view that theism is false.

GRAHAM OPPY

Yes, that is right. A naturalist is going to say that at least as far as the causal stuff goes, all there is the universe. The naturalist position can be more complex than that, but that is the basic idea.

JASON WERBELOFF

Could the universe have non-physical attributes, like psychological attributes, on a naturalist view?

GRAHAM OPPY

There are disputes about who the real naturalists are. Just like there are disputes about who the real atheists are. What I consider to be naturalist is the view that the only minds that there are, are those who have evolved in the history of the universe. There are no minds outside of the universe. Another part of my view is that there is nothing intrinsically worthy of worship.

Both of these views constitute naturalism – not only the view that the universe is all there is, but also that the only minds are those in the universe and nothing is worthy of worship. I am not sure where pantheism falls, whether they are naturalists.

JASON WERBELOFF

Mark thinks pantheism is beyond the pale of rationality.

MARK OPPENHEIMER

I think what is interesting about pantheism is that it requires a commitment to something supernatural. The idea that there is just one entity, that all of us are interconnected does not track with our real-world experience. Although it has a nice, new age, gooey, warm feeling.

JASON WERBELOFF

Pantheism does not hold that there is something supernatural, in the sense that the pantheist thinks that the physical universe and God are identical. And if we really take identity seriously then what you are saying is there are no properties of the physical universe that are not matched by the properties of God and vice versa. If you are talking about something supernatural, that is a mistaken view, since there cannot be anything supernatural on the pantheistic view that is not natural because the natural universe is identical to God.

GRAHAM OPPY

Then there is a question about the distribution of mind, for example. If you agree that the only things that have minds are organisms and stuff that they make, then the universe turns out not to have a mind. By adding a little extra to the definition of naturalism, it will turn out that pantheism is not a type of naturalism.

But it is not clear what is going to hang on having precise definitions at this point. There is a lot of angst around certain parts of the internet about who the atheists are. They are the people who say there is no God or the people who just lack the belief that God exists. I would rather let people use the words however they like and just be clear on what I mean when I am using the words.

Can God Right Past Wrongs?

Sam Lebens

Imagine you a have God - the standard God of your traditional theism, who is benevolent, omnipotent, omniscient. This God creates a world, and he decides to give his creatures, especially his intelligent creatures, free will. It is up to them how they live their lives. But let's also assume that God isn't willing to stand by and let them egregiously abuse that freedom. If he saw an adult abuse a vulnerable child or person, He would intervene since he is too good to let that abuse happen. Imagine furthermore that he wanted humans to be completely free but, simultaneously, never choose bad things. This means that history would be full of only good choices, but each choice was freely enacted.

God then has an idea – He will (provisionally, and against His natural inclination) stand back, watch history unfold, and refrain from interfering. At the end of the process, He will judge the good 'scenes' from the bad 'scenes.'. In the good scenes, the human actors did nice things, and in the other scenes, they did horrible things. Now, let's imagine He has the power to simply delete those scenes. Admittedly, history will now be a bit botched and jolty, although nothing bad will ever have happened. God wants history to make sense, so he decides to retake history, but He keeps the scenes that He liked. So, humans then get to reshoot the scenes that did not go well the first time. Because they have free will, they still mess up, but now maybe more scenes are good. However, there are still some scenes with bad choices and suffering and evil.

He now chooses to do the same thing again: He deletes the bad scenes and starts again. And He does this over and over again until you have a history where nothing bad ever happened, and no bad choices were ever made. In addition, every choice was utterly free.

The question that arises from this thought experiment is how do we know that we're not engaged in some process just like that? How do we know that we are not partway through some kind of cosmic experiment in which several reshoots will guarantee that at the end of time, God will have a history in which free agents always choose wisely and morally?

JASON WERBELOFF

As I understand it, the problem of evil is this: if God exists, and God is the theistic God – so God is all good, all-knowing and all-powerful – then there would not be evil in the world. Why? Because God would have the ability as an omnipotent entity to stop evil. He'd be all-knowing, so He'd know that there's evil. And, since He is all good, He wants to prevent evil from happening. So there would not be evil. And yet, there is evil, so God cannot exist, at least not in the theistic sense. Your solution solves the problem by saying that while there may be evil in the world, this is just one of those scenes that will be edited out later and refilled.

Let me sketch an alternative. My grandmother was dying in hospital, and she was in immense pain. I asked one of the doctors whether he could do anything to alleviate her agony. The doctor said that they could increase the painkillers, but it would have negative consequences. Instead of increasing painkillers, he said I should not worry about it because she will not remember the pain later. The elderly, he said, often have no memory of their experience in hospital. Meanwhile, I was watching her kick under the covers and writhe in pain. I remember thinking that it does not matter that she won't remember this later. The mere fact that it is happening now is a problem.

I wonder whether you don't have the same problem. You say that evil happens, but then it is undone. But I want to say that at some point in time, evil happens, and that is a problem. Your rewinding the tape, and re-recording does not stop that from being the case.

SAM LEBENS

You raise a good question, and it might make my solution to the problem of evil look less attractive. But I think the problem is labouring under some false assumptions, which I will try to expose.

We have to take a step back and ask a prior question: what makes past evils evil? They are gone now. There comes a time where the pain is past pain. But we assume that past pain is still bad. And then, we need an ontology of the past. Ontology is the study of existence, so we need to ask, what exists *now* that makes it the case that past pain is bad?

Some philosophers will have a difficult time explaining what makes the bad events from the past still bad. A group of philosophers called presentists believe that the past does not exist and only the present exists. One problem they have is the problem of explaining how past tense sentences can be true. What makes this conversation we are having true right now is that there is a concrete fact. There is a tangible way that space-time is arranged that we describe as the occurrence of a conversation. This conversation is in the present. However, what makes it the case that a dinosaur walked past this location millions of years ago? The presentists will struggle to answer that question since they believe the past no longer exists. What makes it the case *now*? We feel that there should be something now that makes it the case because if the past does not exist, and the present is all you have got, then it must be the world itself that makes some descriptions of the past true and some false. Therefore, presentists have a problem.

I am not a presentist; I believe that the past is a real place. But I am not committed to that about the future – the future is completely open. Because the future is completely open, there is a real sense in which the future does not exist. The notion that the past exists, but the future does not, is known as the 'Growing Block Theory of Time'. So, time itself grows over time.

Some philosophers, like me, are uncomfortable saying that time grows over time. This is because time measures growth –my children grow over time. Time itself cannot grow over time. Some philosophers, like me, talk about 'hypertime'; this is a complicated sounding word for another dimension over the course of which time grows. So time grows throughout this thing called hypertime. However, at any given moment, time has a certain length. Throughout hypertime, time grows. The outer edge of this growing block called time is the present, and everything inside the block is the past. The past is a real place – but we just do not have a time machine, so we cannot go there.

What makes your grandmother's past suffering such a terrible blight on the universe, is that it is still there. If you could take a time machine back, you would see her still in the pain you saw her in. That pain did not go anywhere. The only thing that changes is that you are now somewhere else in time – you are now in the present, so you do not have to see it now.

The problem of evil is a really, really bad problem. Because not only is the world currently full of evil, and God is just watching, but that pain is still there in the past. However, in my view, once it has been erased, the pain and suffering are nowhere. What makes past evils so bad is that they are forever being replayed. The difference with 'hyper past evils', which is what I call the bad scenes once they've been cut from history, is that once God really has cut them away from history, they are literally nowhere. Therefore, it is a misanalogy to compare the past, even the forgotten past pain of a human being, with *hyper* past pains. I am not willing to say what many theists are willing to say, namely, that God was happy, allowing temporary evils to exist. But there's a difference between temporary evils and hyper temporary evils.

For me, temporary evils still exist; they are just in the

past. But 'hyper temporary evils' are a different matter, and this is what Tyron Goldschmidt and I argued for in our paper, 'The promise of a new past.' We argue that it is at least possible that the pain, suffering and evil around us are merely hyper temporary events. It will hyper-one-day-be-the-case that, once God is finished editing history, that there will hyper-never-have-been any bad. You won't be able to get into your DeLorean and travel back in time and get out to see bad things happening. Bad things won't be happening; bad things will not exist in the past.

MARK OPPENHEIMER

One way of thinking about the future is that it branches. All these different possible worlds could exist, depending on the choices that we make. It seems like what you have is a branching theory of the past. So what happens is, there is a perfect past, or maybe a couple of equally good pasts. And God says he will just be doing retakes until we remove the imperfect ones. Then God will have his perfect book or perfect film. He can just erase all the imperfections, and then there are no longer any branches – just the final product.

I wonder then what you think about the classic time

traveller case, where the person wants to go back and shoot Hitler in the head before the Holocaust happens, thereby saving all those people. One of the objections to this case is that it is logically impossible. The past is the way it is, and you cannot change it. In the same way, we can think about a novel in its final form – it is the way it is, and there is no way that Romeo and Juliet do not die in that particular novel.

But what you do that is so interesting is to claim that we are not in a complete novel – instead, we are in a drafting phase. Like when Shakespeare is thinking about the different ways his novel can play out, he has all these simultaneous unedited drafts sitting around the table. There will be the definitive Romeo and Juliet at some point in time, but all the drafts do not count.

In some sense, we accept that there is a definitive version of a book. Sometimes you have revised editions of a book, and then there might be two definitive editions of a book, and that is okay. But all the other drafts do not count. However, when we claim that the Holocaust never happened since God will edit it out in the future book, then you become this interesting denier of horrible things. You say, 'don't worry, none of this stuff counts – it's all temporary and imaginary'. I start to wonder about that. You are making an interesting metaphysical claim about what counts as reality, in the sense that there are all these drafts. Because they're immoral, these drafts don't have an ontological status. And also, there seems to be a denying going on about things that we currently think of as bad.

SAM LEBENS

Two problems regularly arise with theists trying to defend God in the face of evil. One problem is, they make God out to be not as good as we thought he should be. Tyron and I, in 'The promise of a new past', where we advanced this response to the problem of evil, approvingly cite the atheist philosopher Stephen Maitzen. On the standard free will defence, God gave us free will, and He values us having free will. So, most of the human evil in the world can be explained away in terms of *our* bad choices rather than God. This is because God gave us free will, and now it's our fault, not God's fault. Maitzen rightly dismisses this idea because, what sort of God would say, "Oh, well, I wish I could intervene to save the poor, vulnerable child being abused, but the free will of that abuser is just so important"?

One of the pitfalls of defending God in the face of the problem of evil is that, while God is claimed to be all-loving and all-good, He does not look like he is. The free will defence describes a very strange benevolent God. Another pitfall is that defenders of God tend to deny the reality of evil. One proponent of this view is Leibniz, who insists that the world we live in right now is the most perfect of all possible worlds. That seems like either a failure of imagination or like the moral failure of belittling the very real evil that is all around us.

Tyron and I don't want to deny the reality of the pain and suffering around us. To do so would be philosophically dubious since we know that pain and suffering are real. It is also unethical to endorse a defence that comes at the expense of denying the reality of the pain and suffering around us.

In response to whether this God is good, the answer is that it depends on whether we can make sense of the claim that there will never have been any evil at the end of time. If we can make sense of this claim, then God is not allowing temporary pain and suffering as a prize worth paying for human freedom. He's allowing what we call 'hyper temporary pain and suffering', that is, pain that *will* one day never have happened. And I think that this God is at least a nicer God than the God of the classical free will defence.

To answer the other side of your problem, whether we have not somehow denied the reality of the pain and suffering, I want to, again, say no. In this moment of 'hypertime', the pain and suffering are very real. We have to recognise that it is a hyper temporary reality – a reality that is hyper simultaneous with our current experience. We also have to acknowledge that it is going to leave some imprint on the final history. Because another problem that you could raise with some theodicies is that they may inspire an attitude known as quietism. One of my heroes, Martin Luther King, in one of his speeches, says, "We'll continue on in the knowledge that unearned suffering is redemptive." While those are inspiring words, there is actually a dark underside to them. This dark underside to them is that they could lead some people to invite pain and suffering, since pain and suffering are good for us in the end.

Likewise, my own defence could lead people to say that it does not matter what bad things we do since God will give us another chance anyway. So I might as well live a life of evil debauchery in the interim because God will give us another chance. And that is worse than quietism. It is inviting terrible life plans. Well, no. If we lead terrible lives, it might be that in the ultimate cut of history, we are not there at all. This is because all our scenes can be cut seamlessly if we are bad.

Think of Mike Leigh, the British film director, who has a method where he gets all the actors together, gives them some ideas, and gets them to improvise. Then they improvise again and again. He takes notes and tells them what he likes and what he does not like, and they continue to improvise. Then, eventually, he actually gets to writing a script. In the end, nothing makes it into the script that he does not want to be there. He renders the improvised storyline into a coherent storyline and might add a few bits. I imagine God could do a similar thing: eventually, to fit together all the scenes he wants to fit together, he will have to write a script. But the final cut of this script will take into account all of the improvising that we did in the previous scripts. And so, we want to be careful, even at this interim stage, because the things we do will have an impact on what is ultimately done in the final cut.

To summarise: I don't undermine the reality of our hyper temporary pain and suffering that is really happening now. I also don't legitimise an attitude that says that we can do whatever we want this time around since God will give us subsequent takes.

JASON WERBELOFF

We are trying to push this question of whether evil has happened in this ultimate cut of history. And you are trying to argue two things. You say that evil has happened in a meaningful sense, but not in significant enough a sense to disprove the existence of God. I worry that there is a fallacy of ambiguity happening here, where you are trading on these meanings of 'have happened'.

Going back to the problem of evil, which says that 'If God exists, then evil would not occur'. The problem of evil does not say, 'If God exists, then at the end of time, if we look backwards, it would have been the case that nothing bad happened.' I worry that you are deliberately responding to a weaker version of the problem of evil when the stronger version remains untouched.

SAM LEBENS

I would say that the stronger version of the problem asks, 'Why is there evil *right now?*' Tyron and I are, to some extent, satisfied with the free will defence as a response to that problem. We take Stephen Maitzen to have shown that the free will defence would be an okay response to the more substantial problem of evil – the problem of evil enunciated in the present tense. But it leaves over this other problem of evil: when we look back at the end of time, that God stood by and allowed these evils to happen in the name of free will. We answer by saying that that problem is obviated, as long as God will one day make it the case that no evil ever happened. The evil that is happening right now is justified in terms of some process. The free will defence says that that process is our freedom. Tyron and I say that is not good enough – no good God would just stand by and allow terrible evils to happen in the name of the freedom of the perpetrators of those evils.

But what if the free will defence has not adequately described the process, and the process happens throughout hypertime, not just the course of history. If that is the case, then we can say that what justifies the problem of evil *now* is that it is a process that is unfolding. But the process is not merely historic, it is a hyper historic process. If that is what is happening, it is a question of what process could possibly justify the presence of evil right now?

JASON WERBELOFF

I'm prepared to agree that you've improved on the free will problem. But the free will defence does not cover all evils; it only covers evils that result from our free will. But there are also natural events, like earthquakes. You cannot argue that those evils are happening as a result of free will. Your solution only resolves one type of evil.

SAM LEBENS

To improve the free will defence is already a good thing. I am open to the possibility that theism cannot answer the problem of evil with just one response. We need to consider different types and occurrences of evil. Some evil might be punishments for sins committed, although it would be impossible to say when this is the case. It would be a terrible ethical vice and a theological error to proclaim when evils are punishments. It could also be that some evils are there to refine the people who suffer – that is called the

Irenaean response to the problem of evil, named after St Irenaeus. Like Martin Luther King, St Irenaeus believed that pain and suffering are one of the tools that God uses to sculpt and carve human beings into greater versions of themselves. Pain and suffering can be seen as redemptive. In the Jewish tradition, that's known as 'the pangs of love'. Maybe, in some cases, the divine intimacy theodicy is correct, which holds that some types of pain and suffering bring the sufferer closer to God. I think that the true theodicy will be a mixed bag that brings different defences and theodicies to explain the occurrence of different historical evils.

The free will defence can only answer why some evils occur, and if we have improved on that, then that is already a good thing for the theist. The free will defence cannot explain why natural evils occur, like earthquakes and pandemics. The free will defence cannot explain away those evils. Some natural evils are the fault of humans, like climate change. It might be that not many past natural evils are caused by humans, but we can foresee some horrible natural catastrophes that will be the consequence of bad choices on behalf of consumers and policymakers.

Tyler and I propose the 'divine proofreader response' to the problem of evil, which casts God in the Mike-Leigh-director-role of an ongoing process. This response, we think, can even make sense of natural evils. God would be horrible if He just threw in an earthquake to see how people respond. From God's point of view, the pain and suffering of the earthquake will not make the final cut. But it could be that the occurrence of the earthquake might cause human actors to do some good things with our freedom we would not have thought to do otherwise. And maybe those free choices remain in the final cut. This shows that our revised free will defence could plausibly explain how natural evils occur. God looks really terrible until you realise that God is taking a different kind of temporal perspective -- He is already looking at the final cut. None of these things ever happened in the final cut, but the goods that came out of them might leave a lasting trace on the timeline in the end.

Gabriel Citron from Princeton is a Jewish philosopher of religion. He wrote a paper where he said that, for all we know, this whole world could be a dream. And this dream would be a nightmare. It could be that we will wake up in a world in which there was never any suffering. Tyron and my response is different from Gabriel's – I do not take much religious comfort from the possibility that all of this could be a dream. However, I think you could fairly accuse Gabriel and Tyron and myself of belittling the reality of pain and suffering. Gabriel might agree with Jason about us falling prey to the fallacy of equivocation. But I think he would want to say that we do not deny the reality of pain and suffering. When you are having a nightmare, it is horrible. The question is whether you suffered? From your woken up perspective, you would say, 'it was just a dream'.

I am not sure it is fallacious – we really are suffering right now, and we have made some really terrible choices in our past. But does that mean it will always be the case that we have bad things in our past? The answer is not necessarily. If theism is true, then there is a possibility that we are midway through this process I have described.

MARK OPPENHEIMER

Imagine this: we have a brilliant director who makes family-friendly films. In every movie, people do compassionate, loving things, and nothing bad ever happens. There is no suffering or pain for any of the characters. It is a perfectly G-rated film. When we ask how the movie was made, we find out that the director used the Mike Leigh approach – he says, do whatever you like, chop up some kids, we'll put in some volcanoes and earthquakes, and we will have some mass slaughter. Then I will just cut everything that does not get the G-rating. What is filmed is the horrible triple-X movie– filled with so much pain and suffering and despair. The final product, however, is like a Disney movie – so beautiful.

The question is: If we think about the moral assessment of this director, then we could conclude that this person is the epitome of evil, a monster. And I wonder if that is what your proofreader God is like.

SAM LEBENS

That is a strong objection. But there are two important aspects to highlight in response to this.

Mike Leigh put his actors through what they went through. And, just because scenes got cut does not mean that those actors did not experience the things they were put through. If Mike Leigh somehow ended up with this beautiful G-rated movie with horrific scenes of brutal torture cut from the film, it does not also entail that they were cut from reality. At this point, the analogy between Mike Leigh and our divine proofreading God comes apart. We have a model of hypertime, called hyper presentism, according to which the hyper past is not a place. Just like the presentists think that the past is not a place, the hyper presentists thinks there is no such place as the hyper past.

A consequence of the model that Tyron and I have put forward is that once God cuts the scene from the past, it is literally nowhere. The past does not exist. To use philosophical terminology, it can be described *de dicto*. You can explain what happened in it, but you cannot even name it. It cannot be picked out *de re* because it did not occur. The first part of my answer to your question is that the God that I am describing is importantly unlike Mike Leigh, because this God can make it the case that those scenes were never even shot. Those scenes did not happen, even though they do leave an imprint on the content of the final film in some weird counterfactual way.

The second thing to note is we judge Mike Leigh and the product of his filmmaking activities. We judge him primarily aesthetically when we look at the film. We ask 'Is this a good film'? But, we can also judge Mike Leigh morally. We can ask whether he engaged in immoral behaviour in the making of the film. I have defended the God of my picture from the claim of immorality on the basis that, from His perspective, it will be the case that none of these events ever occurred. Mike Leigh cannot do that trick – he cannot make it the case that his actors never went through terrible pain. So, I can perhaps get God off a moral hook that you cannot get Mike Leigh off.

But, the other part of my response to you is that, importantly, it is not clear that we will use the same criteria to judge God's output that we use to judge Mike Leigh's output. When I watch Mike Leigh's films, it will not be important to me whether these actors freely chose their lines. Many people enjoy Mike Leigh's movies without knowing the process behind the film. The freedom of the actors is not necessarily a part of our evaluation of the aesthetic merit of the film. Rather, we will want to know if the movie was exciting, if it had a good plot, if it moved us. The question is, how are we going to evaluate God. What makes God a good God and His product a good product? It is not important to me that history is exciting – instead, it is important to me that history is an expression of the free will of the beings that God created. But, it is also important to me that God does not allow history to contain terrible gratuitous pain and suffering.

If you put these responses together – that Mike Leigh cannot actually make things disappear and that God is not making a film, but a universe – it follows that there will be a different system of values to judge the product of a director.

JASON WERBELOFF

I have a problem for you: I can follow your line of argumentation but in the wrong direction. In any given situation, I choose the bad choice that results in bad consequences. If I do that, it seems like you are saying I have the freedom to do that, but that my choice will be removed in the final cut of history. In a critical sense, my free will is edited out in the final cut, in the same sense that you are using it to dismiss the existence of evil in the final cut.

SAM LEBENS

One way I could illustrate that you still have a

substantial degree of freedom is that the goods you do in the final cut, even though it's predetermined that you're only going to do good, are really not of God's authorship. In a sense, people who believe that the future is open and believe that humans have free will, along with a group of theologians called open theists, tend to believe that, if God exists, He could not know the future. Because if He knew the future already, there would be a strong sense in which the future already exists. And if the future already exists, there would be a strong sense in which you do not have the power to do otherwise.

I do not want to take a stance on whether God knows the future. But, for the sake of argument, let us imagine that God cannot know the future, and the future is open. If we assume that for the sake of argument, and think from the point of view of my model of time and hypertime, then God actually will only know one thing about the end. He knows that the final cut will only contain good choices – He will have no way of predicting what you will do with your life. That indicates to me in a strong sense that you have freedom. You do not have the freedom to leave an eternal stain of debauchery on the final timeline since a good God will not give you that freedom. Does that mean you are not free? If the God of open theism, who is still omniscient, could not predict what your lifeline will look like in the end, that strikes me as having freedom in a way that is worth fighting for.

MARK OPPENHEIMER

Does it make sense for us to ask for forgiveness for the bad things that we do? If we imagine that God has set in place a series of norms, and we trespass those norms, is it sensible to ask for forgiveness since none of these sins will make the final cut?

SAM LEBENS

One of the things that you do not have much choice about is that you will be living your life until you die. Even if my defence is correct, and you will eventually get another take, it seems to be in your hyper temporary interest to make your life as coherent, meaningful, pleasant and moral as it can be. The moral things you do can last into hyper eternity.

Moreover, if you have done bad, that badness is on your conscience until the next take of history, and therefore asking for forgiveness strikes me as making sense. It might also be that sinners might burn for all eternity in take one. For all we know, putting sinners in hell forever might be a demand of justice. The good people, including the penitent, go to heaven forever. And there might *still* be a second take. It sounds contradictory, but it is not. Repenting is still very much in your personal interest if the demands of divine justice are the existence of a hyper temporary hell. A hyper temporary hell could still last for an eternity, just not a hyper eternity.

Tyron and I also talk about 'light editing' and 'heavy editing'. Light editing is when there is an easy cut – you can cut out the scene seamlessly and retake it in any number of ways. You could shoot that scene multiple times. Some of the edits will be more difficult to make since good and bad choices are sometimes interwoven with one another, and God might want to save a good deed, even though the good deed might be a response to something terrible that someone did. One way that God might save the spirit of the good that you freely did is what Tyron and I call 'heavy editing'. This is where He writes a script for how you must act, without freedom, thereby programming you to say certain things. But the script is inspired by the good that you did in a different story (i.e., in an earlier draft). It could be that the act of penitence is such a tremendously virtuous act that God will have a way of salvaging something of the virtue of that act in the final script, even if it will no longer be repentance. But everything points to Mark having to fast this Yom Kippur.

JASON WERBELOFF

I have a different problem here. Let's say I choose not to fast on Yom Kippur – the Jewish Day of Atonement. I haven't fasted on Yom Kippur for several years. But I hyper-will-have-fasted on Yom Kippur because God will rewrite history until I fast. When He rewrites, I think an evil has occurred. I have made that 'wrong' choice of not fasting, and in censoring that choice, I believe God has committed an evil since there is something good about allowing us to perform even a wrong action. If you remove the record of that choice, it is akin to censorship. If we push the editing idea, what is effectively happening is the editor removes all swear words from a manuscript against the author's wishes. The swear words in the manuscript add authenticity, and it seems like you commit an evil when you remove something authentic.

SAM LEBENS

First of all, let me address the authenticity issue. It might be taking the analogy of the filmmaker too seriously if we judge as 'inauthentic' removing a record of a hyper past sin. 'Authenticity' is one of the values we might use to judge a good movie. Whether the demand for authenticity applies in the same way to judging the final cut of the universe's history is not immediately apparent. There is value in authenticity outside of movies. It is not clear to me whether, in this particular case, something more than an aesthetic loss has occurred.

It is a shallow move for God not to intervene with a person abusing a child on the grounds of censorship. You have a legitimate concern, nevertheless. But your concern does not apply in all cases. It does not seem to apply in the case of someone abusing a child; it might apply to someone eating on Yom Kippur. If God intervenes with someone eating on Yom Kippur, then it is an attack on your freedom. But perhaps this conversation now leaves the realm of philosophical theology and goes into Jewish philosophy now. The question then becomes how we understand the badness of purely ritual sins like not eating on a particular day of the year. And those might not be straightforwardly moral sins, even in my worldview that gives Yom Kippur more metaphysical and theological significance.

But I think it is still consistent with my view that God would judge someone eating on Yom Kippur as only harming God Himself, who can handle the affront. Maybe God will leave the ritual sins on the record because taking them off would really be interfering with a person's freedom for an insufficiently good reason. This seems like a victimless crime, and God might not interfere with victimless crimes or even mild evils. It might be that God allows some threshold of evil. However, it seems that in this particular take of history that we are in now, we have gone way beyond any reasonable threshold. Leibniz is not right – this is not the best history there could have been.

MARK OPPENHEIMER

It strikes me that we now have a situation where we have to figure out which bullets we will bite. We have spoken about the virtues of your account, and it solves some problems of the problem of evil. Your view, however, requires us to bite other bullets. On your take,

God is really a divine censor, and that will make us uncomfortable. What we end up with is Groundhog Day, where you get to lead whatever life you like, rape and murder as many children as you want, but in the end, it won't matter because we will just edit out all the bits that are not G-rated. Your authentic life is going to be quashed because of this censorship concern. We now have to work out in what kind of finished universe we want to live, how much freedom we will have, and make some ultimate value judgements about that best state of affairs. We have to ask questions like: Do we prioritise freedom? Do we prioritise censorship? Do we prioritise suffering? Do we prioritise a beautiful final product? We have to ask about which bullets we are going to bite. Thomas Sowell says there are no solutions, only trade-offs. It might be that there is no way to get to a perfect answer since you are dealing with something nebulous, like value. No answer will satisfy everyone – there will always be someone uncomfortable with any solution we arrive at.

SAM LEBENS

This model, where God can change the past multiple times, which I call the 'scene changing theory of time', is compatible with many different ways in which you might seek to calibrate the values you mention. It is not inevitable that God will cut everything bad out. And it is challenging for us to find that calibration, and there might not be a clear answer or consensus.

But the theory at least gives the Creator some leeway – He does not have to censor everything. I take Jason's point about feeling attacked by a censoring God. But, there is still a robust sense in which the end product is one in which humans have unpredictable freedom. So while something has been taken away, it is not clear how much has been taken away.

This is the perfect segue to speak about Peter Van Inwagen's distinction between a theodicy and a defence. A theodicy is a fully-fledged attempt to explain precisely why an omnipotent, omnibenevolent and omniscient God has allowed evil to occur. I don't think I have a theodicy because it is a highly audacious claim to say you know why God allows these things for both epistemic and moral reasons. What I am offering is a defence. A defence, says Van Inwagen, goes like this: For all we know, this could be why God is allowing evil. And, if the 'for all we know' is true, you have fundamentally undermined the problem of evil without offering up a theodicy. A defence says, 'I don't know why God allows terrible things, but here is a good reason why he might'. And if you've got a perfectly good reason why He might, you've already undermined the sense in which the problem of evil is proof against the existence of God because you have shown that there is a possible world in which a good God allows these evils to occur. So I do not claim to know that there will be multiple takes of this history. I just claim that for all we know, it might be true. And since it might be true, the problem of evil isn't in and of itself a reason to reject the truth of theism. The existence of evil still counts as counter-evidence of theism, but I just don't think it can raise to the status of a logical proof against theism.

About the Authors

Graham Oppy is Professor of Philosophy and Associate Dean of Research at Monash University and serves as CEO of the Australasian Association of Philosophy, Chief Editor of the *Australasian Philosophical Review*, Associate Editor of the *Australasian Journal of Philosophy*, and serves on the editorial boards of *Philo*, *Philosopher's Compass*, *Religious Studies*, and *Sophia*.

Sam Lebens is associate Professor in the philosophy department at the University of Haifa. He is also an Orthodox Rabbi and Jewish educator. His first book was a study of Bertrand Russell's evolving theories about the nature of meaning. His second book is a study in the analytic philosophy of Judaism.

JASON WERBELOFF is a science fiction author with a PhD in Philosophy. He has published over a dozen novels, and co-hosts the *Brain in a Vat* Philosophy YouTube channel with Mark Oppenheimer.

MARK OPPENHEIMER studied philosophy at the University of Cape Town. He is a practicing advocate at the Johannesburg Bar, and has appeared in the Supreme Court of Appeal and the Constitutional Court.

Printed in Great Britain
by Amazon